Kingdom

Kingdom

Jeffrey Perkins

Copyright © 2020 by Jeffrey Perkins
All rights reserved.

This book may not be reproduced, in whole or in part, in any form (beyond that copying permitted by Sections 107 and 108 of the U.S. Copyright Law and except by reviewers for the public press), without written permission from the publishers.

Book design by Drew Burk.
Cover design by Richard Siken.

ISBN 978-1-948510-36-3

Spork Press
Tucson, AZ
SPORKPRESS.COM

To my parents, sisters, lovers, and friends,
and to Lucie. xo

Kingdom

I

KINGDOM

Past the last barn, out a half mile in the green
thick of tended wild, a flight of wind scales
leaves, conjuring a country before land filled.

A boy stands out trying to stop his heartbeat
to find a fawn in the deep moment between
claps of storm and hum of nearby highway.

A subtle tone sounds underneath the kingdom
of whatever the eye can see. Look for the broken
line of starlings in the low June sky.

Imagine a sea of their bodies in murmuration
over these open fields—it was like that.
Then we shot them from the air.

FARM HANDS

Underneath the boy's farm was another one with three sons
who rose early and helped their father, always.

Mornings, the boy crawled down to listen to them feed calves.
Alex liked the feel of tongues and let them have his fingers.

Tom was quick. A rabbit. His wall jammed with ribbons.
He rarely listened to anything except his long feet.

Mark would talk about the lives of trees and what he learned
from *National Geographic*. (Some of them began before Jesus.)

The boys slept in bunk beds, beneath his room. He could hear them
whisper about where they'd go when they left. California.

One night, the room grew quiet. He imagined them wading
into the Pacific with their long boards, tight rubber suits zippered.

Everything rippling out of them.

CADETS

The dusk sky deepens to cave,
Sharp barrage of thunder sounds,

The children only want escape
While father pushes them to edge.

Animals must learn a cage
So he keeps them firm at work

Slowly snuffing a yearn to dash—
Too dim and limp to run away.

When sky devolves to rapid hail
That father leaves his children there

Believing they should learn a rash
Of god acts, sparing any bond

The small ones feel in mother's care—
Boys must learn a tighter lair.

LOVE IN A VACUUM

By the bathtub at thirteen,
the first drops hit the floor,
remember the first flood under

all the pressure. It was too much
to bear, making him a slave
to the chore, the eerie quiet before.

A body rushing outside itself
a way to open a new door
remember the first flood under

pressure. It seemed so rare the peace
that came from wanting more,
that eerie quiet before a storm.

He fell into deeper layers
of his body, touched its core.
Remember the first hot flood—
the eerie quiet before.

BLOODLINE

Not long into this Saturday we uncover a slim bone,
                               then cow skull with dull teeth.

      Clawing at the roots of this crab grass, we tear at the weeds
      attacking the tough stalks

      and flick the unwanted dirt back

until a treasure of bone pieces appear.

My sisters dust the bones
      and blow into the artifacts
      then we label the bones with words.

We set them in a family of objects on the surface road
where pick-up trucks fly into fields through the late months.

We think naming the bones will bring them
into our world.

So when our father tells us to rebury the remains
we believe we have a claim.

Though this is not true
since we are only his, and less, mostly girls.

FIRST JOB

Shallow July. Sweat
in his eyes.

Running the corn stalks.
Dry leaves cut.

His bare feet slap dirt.
Dirt in his teeth.

He comes home with a rush
under his skin.

(Fourteen? fifteen?)
Money in his pocket.

To the hay barn
where he can be alone.

An insect shrieks,
welcoming him—

to the way it is.

He climbs the bales
and presses his body into

the fresh cut of them.
This is where Jesus began, they say.

In the sweating hay
meant for cows.

LEARNING THE ROPES

They do it in the trees mostly
and at the beach, in the sunroom
and in the cellar. His mother's
kitchen and in the corn, just off

the road and in the pool. After
he cuts the brush, during and
after a swim. In his truck back
at his office. By the bed, back

of the garage, empty red shed
by the bee hive and blackberry
patch, the boss always wins.

I WANT STRAIGHT A'S IN ALL POSITIONS

The way it worked was he'd grunt
when I finished an act and I'd hear
a grade—D, B, D, C, F.

How I undid his Don't Mess
with Texas belt buckle; how I
unbuttoned his wide-plaid shirt.

Later, I would reflect on my practice
and techniques. My goal to balance
nuance with ambition.

I wanted to bring him to tears,
move him into groans until
I couldn't understand anymore.

I know it will sound in me like air
inside a hollow drum—just before—
it's struck wide open.

EIGHT YOUNG MEN, 23 TO 24 YEARS OLD

After Shine, I follow him to the fourth floor
in the South End where the Pru rises behind
the brownstones—evoking 1970-something.

Paul just saw Pussycat Explosion so Eric puts on
Christina. A red shiny belt around his slight
waist. A large plasma TV is mounted

above a faux fire that's always on. A puppy jumps
on our laps with his manatee toy, wanting us to pull.
Someone has to lose his pants so Leo loses his

and then Eric. Max undoes my belt. Nobody has
much body hair. Designer underwear is everywhere.
Usually, everybody's high but Randy's in rehab,

so we're starting late. It happens in our centers—
this mutual calculation and re-calibration
to give something away.

CONTEMPORARY ART MUSEUM

Coral reef of buttons. A bale of toothpicks. Pins.
Clouds of styrofoam cups and drinking straws.

My date's English halts and repeats
buttons, buttons. Buttons. They are buttons!

In the bathroom God says, I'm going to be honest—
what it will take to turn this life is great.

A collection of 5,000 empty clam shells
from the beaches of Nova Scotia.

It began while we weaved
our way back down.

His allergic reaction to lunch became small hills
I run my fingers along.

A sea is behind the snow we look at
from the closed café. Somewhere the waves swell.

Somewhere a landscape becomes light.
Somewhere it's plowed. Salted.

BREAKFAST IN MALIBU

Everything here
ends in the ocean
whether you know it or not.

At the Hideaway
J and I talk about the revolutionary nature
of words and his new French girl.

At dinner, his hand snakes the table
spooning her fingers.
She's so swell, he says, driving home.

Later, in his bed
he calls it love.
This infatuation.

ARMY OF LOVERS

Believe artists want you
as lovers, dream of you
from lofts above rivers.

Photographers, installation
artists who build new cities
at dusk in secret alcoves.

A world of smooth skin
designers with long slender
noses. Homes on the Hudson.

They will walk you under
bridges too late at night.
Intoxicate your slender will.

Then Tokyo! Stockholm!
The awkward Maldives.
(Beware these advances.)

Alone in a stunning green,
their landscapes become
all you can imagine now.

ALMOST EMPTY IN THE CHAMBER

In the hollow of the foot between the links of spine
in the space between the fledging plant and weed

when the birds go quiet before the summer storm
under the car's seat back of the couch pillow
between the blue blouse and the jeans on the line

after the switch clicks but before the light bulbs
when the cigarette burns out from the toss
when an ice cube tightens in its small pool
when the last guest leaves all the plates alone

between boats floating before the motor floods
when the fuel rests before it catches in the night.

THE SQUIRREL

I let him in late one night.

He wouldn't settle down—
frozen still then suddenly manic,
a tiny pounding squirrel heart.

I found almonds in the closet
arranged a few in a gold rimmed dish
placed it in the corner by the ficus.

After weeks of darting in and out
he began to trust our little home;
perhaps it was the occasional glass of Merlot.

I started calling him names:
my little darling, Speedy Gonzales, bunny bunny.
I forgave his teeth, his endless gnawing.

One morning during breakfast,
his dry nuts and my poached eggs,
I noticed his heartbeat slowing.

I invited him into my bedroom that night—
told him stories until we fell asleep,
curled together in my little bed.

The next day, I couldn't stop smiling.
I wrote him a note and left it with the nuts;
I wanted to discuss our future.

He never came home.
I stayed at the door that night calling for him—
chipmunk, my love, little bunny.

II

MENU

It began with miso and mussels,
slurping dribble of slight sea stones
opening in a swirling broth, without
diction—murmurs and whispers in a great bowl.

It began in these soft places—subtle flash
of recognizing kind across a wide table,
in the tight skin of a neck. The desire
to gather and take a step closer.

CRUSH

                a hot March
kills the coat check line

        sweet Jesus
                Hallelujah!

        grabbing at the lacquer shine
            I flute
                    your name

            (do you get where I'm going?)

                    stars

                Baker   Buffalo

        Rattlesnake
Rock.

SPRINGTIME IN TEXAS

I have a photo of you, looking out
before we knew how we worked.

Outside the Alamo among little bridges,
you were the boy who kept the secrets.

Bars lined the river. We ate on its edge.
Boats licking stones. We swam on a roof.

A city stood above where I fell for you.
Walking without coats. Smelling the air.

Then Austin—our room above the Congress
Avenue Bridge. (The giant bed.) A wall of windows.

Tourists gathered below to watch bats.
I could only make out the shadows.

Little figures looking up, hoping to see
something swarm.

LAST DAY OF SEPTEMBER

Two men and one striking woman
with warm olive skin and long black hair
like the sheen of a seal. One of the men
strips to a Speedo while the other
wears his coat. The woman balances purple
sunglasses off the bridge of her nose.

They drink wine and eat feta with fresh
French bread. Bottles of champagne empty.
They call to the seals but the light
tires too soon. The campers move back.
The fishermen go home. Light leaves
night air. They gather driftwood

and blast their music and light a fire.
When the wind rises they miss the barking
seal. To prove they still can, they strip quick
and run—naked into the stone cold sea.
The woman's perfect breasts. The men in love
with one another. The sudden shock of fall.

THE VISITORS

In the mansion, we're assigned to separate rooms.
You are in a slight and beautiful cusp.

It's what I'm after. Wallpaper. In the morning—
when it is not yet—kissing you is like fog.

You play the instrument in a shirt so loose I want
to whisper into each rib.

Every room, a new play. Sometimes a woman wails
through the wall. I wonder what will survive.

I came back later to find the key I left
in the upstairs hallway, sloping in its fine fashion,

but they started singing the chorus and I wanted it
from the beginning.

So, I listened from the porch until they grew quiet,
thinking I might see you among those gathered.

That I might finally get the Saturday night of you
at the last show, before it runs out, into that field.

IN ADVANCE OF LEAVE TAKING
for Margot

You're better at this than I. See it as a new land, a gold thing.
I picture it too quiet. A flickering table at the place on the hill

late into a night when we sit and talk in a dying light too dim
to see whatever's left to eat. High ceilings and then a new bed.

In the morning, I take the flights down fast, like water flows
a finished tub. The Rue de Rome empty except a slight glimpse

of moon through sheets of thin clouds. I find you at the hotel
tucked in your slim twin, your feet close to my absent head.

You are my sister. (Isn't this what you wanted: words in a case.
To be *the* girl.) In the dream I am driving with dad.

We're riding to an auction to mill about the various objects
of some farmer's life—a harrow, misshaped coil of wire, glasses.

I'm ten and torn about whether love is stronger than not—
At the Cape Codder Inn, the soap cakes wear protective sleeves.

It's impossible to finish one, even in a week. The lonely slivers.
In the dream, I'm afraid of the day I will have to say goodbye.

BLACKBIRD

Satya wants to go inside the television
to join the people watching the game.

I explain we can't—the animated screen
is just an illusion. Yes, a baseball game

exists somewhere right now but we can't
get there in time to watch the players

run into that perfect open green field.
Over and locked by the time we'd arrive.

Sometimes when I let myself be quiet,
the idea I grew up with—that life

is always elsewhere—sits down beside me.
The pockmarked kid can't stop moving.

Fear can do amazing things to me—

But walking with you early on a Sunday,
walking Bedford, or even Driggs,

I notice a new detail in the way we walk.
Maybe I can slow this small heart down

like the slight slope up the Williamsburg
Bridge, before you see Manhattan.

Like when I saw you tear up
for the first time, when that song came on.

WHEN YOU PLAY KANYE

I will only bring you joy like the fortune cookie fortune
reminding you the universe is not all ill.

I will help you remember why you love even awkward time
of missed things, so much falling off itself.

Remember we were born on the same day in the most modern hospitals
of interchangeable letters.

Now, stirring yams into pie and building a world of soft tents,
we pin gems onto our wide collars.

I will swallow my pride, my opinions when you need nothing most.
I apologize in every word.

WHEN I WON'T KNOW YOU

In Berkeley, there are signs for a psychic fair.
You want to stop, but I've sworn them off.

I secretly fear we might end then, when someone
says we're through. But you can't find a parking

spot so while you circle the block I go in
and have my aura cleaned. Students murmur I'm blue

or green light circling their hands around my head.
When you finally arrive, we sit in front in folding

chairs and Rachel, twenty one, tells us we were
Romans once: Greased soldiers from different ranks,

one ordering the other to combat, to slip off boots.
We will finish our karmic debts in this lifetime.

There will be no more driving next to you stopping
anywhere for dinner. No more kissing.

YOU ARE IN ANOTHER ROOM

This urge to do whatever can be done
to stop the headlong speed—

to stand tight, courageous against
a thunder of mad grizzlies

driving us steady toward the still,
unguarded moment of dusk.

Even if I marshal every motley
hero to my cause—somehow

convince everyone on earth
to stop moving—the grass will

go damp. The tulip's elastic petals
close. The night will bully the room.

The stars will not hold back.
Sleep pushes in. Yellow grays.

No matter what I desire above
all else, this darling will pass.

AVOIDING THE TOPIC

And the thin one, the beautiful
finch of them, fears what's next

rolling his eyes back into a mislaid
valley—a moth, worm without dirt.

He thinks he can save himself
by cutting the air of conversation

but the question is accustomed
to corners, lying as it does inside

a man's gut, growing on its own meal
of particular logic. Watch. It becomes

a grapefruit—miraculous child—
ruby fruit of thistle. Flowering doubt.

THE NIGHT THE HOUSE WAS EMPTY

You took the matches and all the things I could burn

no beer in the fridge, frozen vegetables thaw
in the dumpster out back.

I climb into the rusted truck
        and no one has anything
        to say anymore.

One day, everything I feared assembled outside my door
and rang the bell on tiptoes. When I answered the creatures
looked up and smiled,

so proud
of what I built, what I never did.

WHEN I COME ACROSS THE PHOTO

of you standing in front
of that tower, the steel
beams of cross purpose—

my lungs lose the air
I don't even want
anymore.

I am the not—the one
not taking anything of you.
Not telling you to look

at me, not adjusting
your collar. The not me
with you—the he—the he

takes that photo—he—
the one who took over
the stories of you.

And then, his arms
around your center—
tight in the blue pool.

In that photo, he's
the subject. And sex
and so much more of it.

BROADENING THE THEME

Imagine no people
next to you
or on the street outside.

Or if you are somewhere no one
already is, then imagine no one
out here or ever in your bed.

It's empty
and so are the chairs in the dining room—
there's no living room to speak of.

All the boats are docked—rise
and fall according to waves, crash
in a storm. The sidewalks melt their snow.

The baseball field is for the birds.
Parking is never a problem.
Traffic lights blink until they go blank.

I forgot how to build a house
no one to hold the board
while I draw the nail. And why do it.

BROOKLYN

In the morning, after they talked through the logistics of returning
        personal items
such as keys, books, and clothes, they sat next to each other on the great
        blue bed.

It was too much to think that this exact moment was the precise end of
        them,
as neither one had seen it coming when the conversation began.

When the door closed (for the last time) a horrible sob could be heard
        inside,
as though a stabbing had taken place but no one would call an ambulance.

Walking down the street the other one looked close at the way the sun
        hits each building,
trying to record how this place looks in spring. His second home.

III

INDEPENDENCE DAY

Father's in the hospital
unable to breathe,
and I'm up all night
having sex with a nymph
who's high on anything but sleep
who asked *where are you going*
when I got up to leave
and I looked back and said,
it's complicated,
there used to be trees here
but we needed boats.
We cut them all down.

HUMAN BEHAVIOR

      You said my eyes change color
and I thought of the black pools
of horses. Their steady gaze,

blank in the face of whatever
they witness us do. (Civil war.
Genocide. An ultraviolence.)

      I wasn't allowed to love them—
unpredictable beasts that can throw you
and break you quick.

No black riding boots. No reckless ride
on blossomed hips through fields.
Do my eyes really switch?

      The losing light of a carnival
in November. A messy split of orange.
Hazel rim murmur of a swarm.

I never fed a horse an apple, never
watched its long mouth seduce the fruit
after a late afternoon ride.

      Maybe my eyes know more than I
about what really excites me. Somehow
sees through what I do to myself.

Watch for their lightening and tell me
when they shift. I'm waiting
to see what you do.

I WENT INTO THE STORM

I went to the room to watch where the rain ended and would begin again.

I went in on purpose.

I went to stop thinking I knew best what was going on inside.

I went into an almost blinding room.

I went into the basic problems—the mother, the rugged father.

I went to pay for what no one wants.

Yes, into the dynamic fixed inside me, the surgical avoidance.

I went into the unexpected—into the rain that stopped and started.

I went into that room so deliberately.

I went inside the opposite of fleckless, brilliant. To the other side— leaving this one for somewhere else.

CLOSE ENCOUNTERS OF THE THIRD KIND

A small army of missing children
from the sides of milk cartons
and World War II airmen walk out
in exchange for one new man.

I'd forgotten how insane Roy Neary
appears to be—unearthing the fleshy
bushes from his yard, throwing them
through the kitchen window, how he

reshapes the mashed potatoes while
his family watches him carve the dense
cloud of white. Teri Garr—that voice—
finds him clothed in the shower.

He walks so willingly into the spaceship.
I can only think of therapy and the son
slamming the bathroom door, spitting.
What it costs to recover a lost father.

Did the child ever make another film
or was he haunted by Richard Dreyfus'
image, walking so gracefully into
the light air of the hovering alien craft?

IN THE LATE SEASON

In the awkward center
of this yellowing room

I may swerve into the beams
of purposeful light as antidote

to this tight-wound rug.
Eating this cherry

can I still strip fruit from pit?
What if my throat receives the stone?

This is what led my mother to say
she was going away,

though she never could
follow through.

Sometimes the space between
the rungs of the blinds were

too wide for her, the teetering
weight of a glass stem,

the faded gloss shine
of the dinner menu against her hands.

She could not touch a fork.
She could not manage.

I'm sorry I could not make
the dinner.

WRITE MY FATHER FROM UKRAINE
for Kirsten

Write father from Ukraine.
Tell him about the taste of tea
and what it means to be alone.

Write father about the pelting
snow. What fierce white is,
how it falls in Autumn.

Tell him how it feels not to ask
someone for what you need
so he can know it

in his field in a New
England town. Let him feel
everything foreign. How

hollow silence sounds
in your room. Write my father
about kissing, how it is

with a stranger. With
a man. Your body feels
a new opening now.

Tell my father about the kids
teaching them the words
for snow, ice skates.

Tell father about
the words missing, after,
lightening.

The sound they make
in Ukraine. When you miss
America and the way sheets

feel against you.
Missing someone you love.
Tell him about that.

When you want to die.
How you imagine it now
in Ukraine among the others.

AFTER EUROPA

A woman on the green line catches my eye. I follow
her onto the wrong train. A strong nose, dirty
blond hair, thick eye brows. Almost a pretty boy.

She takes her hair down when the train leaves
the tunnel into college students, the sun. At the museum
we part. Everything at the salad bar is 49 cents.

It doesn't matter if it's the egg or the chicken. I run into
Larry who first told me to come out to my parents
when I was having problems with Fernando.

In the courtyard there's snow, a thin crust of ice.
One set of footprints out. She reminds me of Jane,
who I locked in the closet when we were kids.

I knew what I was doing. Making her suffer.
I said goodbye to a lover for good this week.
I wanted him myself. I go see Europa—

taken by the bull. The sky turns purple above her
like looking down Boylston into Roxbury this week.
Winter turning against itself. I watch her disappear.

Across the water, riding the bull. I am one of the friends
watching it happen in a fancy dress. Or I am Europa.
Holding on. Kicking the door. Screaming at the man.

LOST TERRITORY

We live for a winter among the people.
Speak to one another about food,
customs, and how we are together now.

I collect our odds in a tiny house—
numbers, dinners, receipts from various
trips to tropical island nations.

Then the wood barn falls into itself.
The central cathedral is left unfinished.
(There will never be enough money.)

Strange how fast a dream becomes yard.
No one on the benches. The statue
loses a limb and ivy, or less, obscures

the plaque of how we were—
how I choose the tight mountain pass
but couldn't look down or the beach

too rocky to swim. Most nights I ate
ceviche looking out at various stages
of late light.

MEMORY DEVICE

I will save the time we saw *The Pillow Book*
on the coffee table.

Our dinner at Ten Tables
on the top shelf of the bedside bookcase.

In the bureau, among my shirts,
I'll save our skinny dip at Loon.

Every discarded oyster shell will reappear
where I toss the change.

When I fetch the towels from the dryer,
the late night showers.

Sipping water from the tap every green glass
of wine reappears.

The ridge of the door's casing will hold me.
(The sugar bowl, our reunion.)

The space between wall and fridge is California.
The ceiling, our Texas.

Inside each cotton ball I'll keep our mornings.
In the dark bulbs—our nights.

THE SMALL BIRD FLIES BRIEFLY INTO MY KITCHEN

Always on his way out
when he enters a room.

Says he can't stay long
so everyone knows

not to build a narrative
around his arrivals. Rather

be glad water rests
before it's poured into glass,

that dishes are held
and then released.

The various condiments say
it's okay to disappear.

When he left this time
everyone said he was going

anyway, had other lives
he was running off to—

a wife, a husband, three kids
in another Sweden.

Hush the din and let him go
way of exits—funnel, sieve,

even this drain. Let him go out
the propped window of my pantry.

He's on another mission now.

SEX, WAR

I want to know the names
of wildflowers. Each one naked

in raw exactitude. A path
of ghost string to find a way back

to this handsome danger;
humbled to find radiance.

Away to a further out field
where we can have a wider sleep.

Build a fire to see even more,
strip at midnight to swim out—

to find the abandoned motorboat.
The slim key begs for its turn.

We didn't lose the war on poverty.
We fled. Loving the hunger instead.

IN THE LAST HOURS OF THE FIX

when the alarm is to call
just before the purr of water
rolls to boil, in the moment
you can still make out the sun
on the plane of trees, when
I almost forget what it was
to cross the Golden Gate Bridge
in that mini-van on our way
to Point Reyes, I catch myself.
Time had its way. When the cellos
begin I'm afraid you might be
in Saskatchewan, where I have
no intention of ever arriving.

THE FINALE

What can be necessary
now?

In the garden after dusk, only mosquitos
keep my arms alive.

              A life run.
(no next)

I lived for moments in a bed
making short noises. (Music!)

Squirrels on the fire escape, a downed ship, then
bye—so many lines can be
(cut)

All adventure stories end—

      I will river out
      in a darkness. Not all opens.

Who wouldn't want an end to this lull?

(where are you going without me?)

THERE WILL BE DANCING

A bird calls the same song for days.
Everything overcast. Living out of
burnt brown suitcases. Dragging ash,

over blue-tiled trays, gray hair thriving
at temples, margarita glasses chipped
on their blue rims. The pear always
before it's ripe. Sing something
else, bird. So many broken umbrellas.

A radio comes on, a baby cries.
It's all enough now. What happens
after the end.

Break all the way down. Stop listening.
Burn the house. Plant a row of trees.
Build a magnificent forest.

Find a new place.

IV

WHAT'S HERE

I ask the sea by walking
into it. Feel its cold wet shock
and still I move.

In the field, mountains hold
the future to a fish caught in a tidal
pool before the sea runs out.

At the edge of the pool a boy
and his sisters play games. One day
a journey. Soup and mud cake.

They record it on audio tape as if
only they survived, interviewing
each other about the wreck.

A muffled hum when I slip
under. Is it in my head or
in this sea?

MIRACLE

Sometimes I wonder if I am only the last substance
I've taken in—the smoke of the Camel Gold cigarette,
the glowing amber of the double whiskey shot.

I sit in the rain until I soak these new clothes,
allow a mold to grow inside my elastic ligaments
to make myself into an unrecognizable body.

I will not drink the vital element, will not breathe
such careful air. I will not dissolve this radiant galaxy
of small mistakes I've made into myself.

MAP OF ATONEMENT

Back then, Sara invited the artists
for rum-spiked punch. I brought
my lover with his colossal German nose.

I almost forgot how they adored him.
How he built a cartilage between them.
Instructing the guests in an essential trick

of how to tip go-go boys. Now, the church
strikes ten, but sounds like twenty.
Unreliable time. I was a fickle lover—

ungrateful. I'm sorry little cosmos
of misters. Alphabets of horse and fox.
May you love one another deeply soon.

Climb those attic stairs and look down.
What do you see when I think of you now—
do you see the wasps? Their yellow.

POEM TO SELF

You do not need to find the way
by chipping off pieces of a statue

and throwing them into a lake.
Let the old you be what it was then

and swaddle it whole. The minor act
of remaking is a species of violence—

what we learn in school—our lack.
What if you were never not?

One day, when you least expect it,
you'll look at the life you remade

and want an arm back. Let the quiet
of the lake be unto itself—mirror.

Let the monument stand and be joined
by an elaborate graffiti.

CONSOLATION

These same words form
inside your mouth. Same o.

Same s of s. The same fire
sparks inside our brains.

In this way, I am with you—
no matter how long

since rain hit the high windows.
Thank you, wise teacher,

for your disappearance.
One's only necessity.

The new world of us is here
in the near invisible thread.

Walking down the street
the wind becomes our sex.

SECOND CHANCE

The party I threw was too packed
for you, though you were having your way
with the guests, telling them the one

about your dream with Whoopi
in which you told her another dream
in which she gave you life advice

to keep moving. Just say yes to it all.
When you were ready to go you took
the youngest one away. Thought he was

too young for me. And there was carrot
cake I made, by the door with a knife.
You sliced into it and took a sliver

for the road. Told me later
it was the best cream cheese frosting
you'd ever had. Cold and rich

like walking down Park on a Sunday
all the lobbies bigger than most places
people sleep, and just to walk through.

The man on the subway said a nickel
would do. You'd be surprised how fast
those little coins add up, he said,

when you've got nothing but empty.
I noticed you slip out, noticed the slight
slice from my cake and the boy gone too.

Thanks for coming back. My hand resting
on your chest feels the air swell up
inside you. (Sweet Jesus.)

Women never tell straight men
they're beautiful. Yes, they've been waiting
for you to spread the word.

REUNION

My head is planted in the mural you plastered across a billboard—
a spectacular summer sequel.

A furious drum beat rises from nowhere, building a savannah—
				making the mantou bread, slash and burn of the daikan
cake, garlic scapes,
	pillows of baby bok choy, fennel—loved animals inside churn.

We crawl from our cave lives
to make a new paste between what became of us.

Rest in the hammock web, above the non-winged ants, elevating
our new shyness.

Disengage your early warning systems. Breathe deeper than feels natural.

All the water has been circulating since the start.
					Bring down the orange coconut
	to drink the sea.

BEAUTIFUL CATASTROPHE

You're a strong wind with designs
on my red surface planet, once inhabited
by nations of peculiar bird species.

I had to lose them to make room
for the move—piling uneven boxes while
making cider donuts in the lime kitchen.

Nina Simone can sure sing the blues
when you're not listening to the words.
Black is the color of my true love's hair.

Someone has to go chop more wood.
I don't want to let that kind of cold
inside this loose fitting shirt.

Okay, you can build a small space station
on my moon. But make it compostable.
Like all the cool kids in Brooklyn.

Let the rain break it down. Sew seeds
into the roof to make a private forest.
We can meet under the new trees.

And the birds will congregate and throb
in the branches, migrate back to us
from their afar. How I love you.

RACCOON MOUNTAIN

He jumps out of a moving car
trying hard to stay alive.

The Silhouette Bar behind us.
A hooded moon on watch.

They'd really love us, he says,
pulling on my cigarette hard.

Just be all about us. Like he is.
Wants to take us himself.

We take his word instead—
get out—head south at dawn.

Past the slow parade of Ohio.
The hills of your Kentucky.

At night, we sleep in a tent
off a long stretch of freeway.

Where we're going the water
moves up quiet at night. Stirs

in the morning. Look out
at the lake. How fast it shifts

underneath. A giant storage
battery. A beautiful machine.

IN THE NEXT GALLERY

I say, let's plant a farm—let rows of corn,
cukes, tomatoes, and winter squash weave

the concrete floor. Raise the dirt into beds
with wood walls. Crack the ceiling until rain

finds a way in. Open blue sky here
in the center of the sheetrocked cathedral.

We can invite the city on embossed invitations.
Tents in the new wing for whomever stays

the night. In the late hours you and I can escape
to the sea compartment and taste the dark salt.

So many lovers we won't meet. Horses left
unrode. Language tapes boxed in the basement.

It's always in other rooms. Your collarbone
under my hand. My air inside your lungs.

WHAT I LEFT FOR YOU

I never went to the top of the Empire State
or on a cruise ship in the Azores.

I never climbed those stairs at the Eiffel Tower,
never sky dove, or made a whiskey sour.

I never slept on a moving train or watched
the light disembark in Japan.

I never held someone in the art book aisle
or searched for least public space in a park.

I never took a shot of tequila after a French kiss,
so one day I could say I did with you first.

Sunday, you and I sat on the roof deck
when the clock began to strike too long.

I made out Orff's *Carmina Burana* in the gongs
and where do you go after that?

I thought blood determined our outcomes
and I never hugged my father goodbye.

History is the past of whatever's left undone.
My father's body is promised to me.

The Greek islands, the Netherlands,
the Nile are for you.

LOVER'S DISCOURSE

We will meet again in a frozen Oslo,
reveal our bodies only after

we spot each other's naked hands
in the post office line, then remember

that skin of finger, bird of wrist,
bringing us to a beach—the glowing arm

of you holding a book, reading pages
that were once alive in a forest in Quebec,

while I, barely open eyes, daydream
of binding your hands in leather

tying your figure to a bed to keep you
because I'm weak for your lucid skin.

Our lives as men, women—all the dreams
we created before we knew about bodies.

Until then, I'll search for you
in the profiles of others in a sparse Wyoming.

Build a land of near misses of your neck.
You will know me by the new book

in the window of the village bookstore,
hinting at distant memories of light.

IN THE DEEP STRINGS

i.

After the blue starvation
the trees' white explosions canopy us out
looking for a new dance.

We long for a quickening—to be sailors
with another logic but you are afraid
of the stories of the shipwrecks at sea.

ii.

Bring your attention to your disasters.
Then—start again.

The caribou will go south
and splurge. Let's follow.

We can make it from this mud thick river.
Ride it down as it grows.

Walk the shallows— remember—
river is only sea missing salt.

Feed on the green until we feel the pull
of new arrangements we could never imagine at the start.

iii.

Suddenly a space inside wants more room—
take off the white shirt and string it out on a wide line—

infinite ways of bending
had to be articulated.

I became mohawked, a lion
in cut off jean shorts.   Let's go.

iv.

On the coast of Maine mermen hold each other up
on the beach—

births, deaths, building bodies from fish.
Mark my words.

We will unbeach
each other one day.

Our body cages will fall.
I don't want to carry this weight any longer.

v.

We are in a boat now, jetting out
                standing on the edge
taking photographs of strong wind.

Inside the under of the ship is a dark wood—
a hallowed cavern of hammocks
with thick circle windows cut into black.

Here, where the dishes are held into the walls,
we make spaghetti.
Patience, darling.

We made it out and now trees
keep us afloat. We have to trust where
the dark bound fibers are leading.

vi.

Sometimes, a life rises up
like morning

starts slow
into a room's crooks

to fill
what doesn't seem possible.

Everything you thought solid   Say it.
is no more.

The gold hue
of rock. The paper thin
echo of leaves.

vii.

There is an island no one visits.
The way lost until we remember
we built it for this purpose. To bring us back.

I forgive it all.

viii.

Let me put my hands where they have
never been before.

Let these eyes witness something
I shouldn't let them see

these ears
a sequined sound to fall in love with.

Let's reclassify the books by their births
or time of sex.

Push it all until it's beyond. Don't hide this revolution.
Donate your sweaters or cut off their arms.

ix.

We'll grow a new world
off the galley kitchen.

A destination for the masses
and all our awkward moments.

What was once firm will fall
as new transplants take root—

Japanese maple, Manchurian linden
American ash—until it smells clean.

The maps from space will not work here.

We will have to find our way
without the aid of satellites.

This is what you've been waiting for.
Welcome home.

KINGDOM COME

In the corner of the dive bar
stands a fresh boy with The End

stitched across his chest. He says
he's been gone for a long time.

An elegant and complex bird
in search of a certain feel of cage.

I just departed my last ship.
It is my ever after time now.

He told me I could have his castle
and his land in all directions.

All I have to do is release this boat,
my unsteady house. Quiet.

The wings disguise themselves
as merely feathers.

Acknowledgements

Grateful acknowledgment to the following publications in which some of these poems first appeared:

The Adroit Journal: "Raccoon Mountain"
The Cortland Review: "In the Next Gallery," "In the Last Hours of the Fix"
Crab Creek Review: "Almost Empty in the Chamber"
Fifth Wednesday Journal: "Lost Territory"
The Fourth River: "Lover's Discourse"
The Massachusetts Review: "Write My Father from Ukraine"
Melancholy Hyperbole: "Farm Hands" and "When I Won't Know You"
Memorious: "Avoiding the Topic"
Mid-American Review: "Kingdom"
Rhino: "Army of Lovers" and "Independence Day"
Rust + Moth: "In the Late Season" and "You Are in Another Room"
The Southampton Review: "Contemporary Art Museum"
Tuesday; An Art Project: "The Squirrel"
Tupelo Quarterly: "Map of Atonement"

Deepest thank you to the following people who supported these poems and this book along the way: Lucie Brock-Broido, Michael Burkard, Gabrielle Calvocoressi, Barb Caruso, Robin Chalfin, Sunu Chandy, Fay Dillof, Kyle Dacuyan, Amy Gerstler, Kirsten Giebutowski, Erich Goetzel, Ralph Hamilton, Marie Howe, Major Jackson, Michael Klein, Timothy Liu, Pam Matz, Kevin McLellan, Susan Merrell, Kathleen Ossip, Margot Pappas, Spencer Reece, Martha Rhodes, Leslie Seldin, Don Share, Jean Valentine, Sarah Wetzel, and all my dear friends.

beenThank you to the creative communities of the Bennington Writing Seminars, the Cambridge Center for Adult Education, the Fine Arts Work Center Summer Program, the 92nd Street Y, and the Vermont Studio Center.

Thank you to Richard Siken and Drew Burk for sending this book into the world.

JEFFREY PERKINS grew up on a farm in New Hampshire and earned his BA from Earlham College in Richmond, Indiana and his MA in American Studies from the University of Massachusetts Boston. He later studied poetry at Bennington College, where he received his MFA and was the recipient of the Jane Kenyon Memorial Scholarship. His poems have been published in *The Adroit Journal, The Cortland Review, The Massachusetts Review, Memorious, Rhino, Tupelo Quarterly*, among other journals. He was a 2019 Artist-in-Residence at The Watermill Center. He is the co-author, with Frances Moore Lappe, of *You Have the Power: Choosing Courage in a Culture of Fear*. He lives in Culver City, California. thekingdompoems.com

CPSIA information can be obtained
at www.ICGtesting.com
Printed in the USA
FSHW021110140620
71169FS